A Book of Nonsense

A Book
of Nonsense

by

MERVYN PEAKE

PETER OWEN · LONDON

ISBN 0 7206 0412 5

PETER OWEN LIMITED
12 Kendrick Mews Kendrick Place London SW7

First British Commonwealth edition 1972
© 1972 Maeve Gilmore

Printed in Great Britain by
Villiers Publications Ltd London

For Elizabeth and Ernest Cromwell Peake

Contents

Introduction by Maeve Gilmore
(Mrs Mervyn Peake)

Non-sense, or Nonsense? Nearly always 'nonsense' seems to make more sense than an income-tax form, or any of the other innumerable documents with which life becomes increasingly laden, so that one's eyes and mind become glazed with non-understanding.

This 'Book of Nonsense' is more understandable to me than filling up a census, and certainly it was to Mervyn Peake, who wrote these poems and the other pieces in the book, from 'The Dwarf of Battersea' to the unfinished 'Adventures of Footfruit', over a period of some thirty-five years.

He was as aware of the foibles, the gentle and the not so gentle absurdities, the make-believe world of human beings, including himself, as a cat who can sniff a mouse, another cat encroaching on its own domain, a dog, or a bird. But his aware-ness was not restricted to his mind alone: snatches of conversa-tion overheard in a bus, a man with a nose the size of a potato, running urgently for a train, and missing it, at Victoria Station, never went unnoticed, and he made jottings on anything handy, such as the inside of a packet of Woodbines, or a menu in a Lyon's Corner House. His own conversation often had a non-sensical element in it. Sometimes this annoyed people; but if they responded, a whole evening might be spent talking a great deal of 'nonsense'.

One day, going to see some friends in an unfamiliar part of London, we stopped to ask the way of a couple walking in the opposite direction. They gave detailed and kindly advice, and it seemed that our walk was to become fairly extensive. After the formal courtesies of gratitude for welcome information, Mervyn said to these strangers: 'Oh, if I had only known, I would have brought my camel.' It did seem funny to me, but I can quite see that to someone else it might have been considered, along with puns, a very low form of humour.

Words were shapes and sounds to him. He saw them, as if

he were listening to an unknown language, in shapes. His childhood in China, where he was born in 1911, had an undoubted influence on all his work – drawing, painting and writing. In the Chinese written characters, for instance, he had imagined a world of pictures, and he always spoke of the great humour of the people who surrounded that part of his life. His father was a medical missionary – one of the 'white devils', as they were called. After many vicissitudes, he earned the respect and love, not only of his fellow-missionaries in the compound, where the Peake family lived, but of the local mandarins, and the coolies who were part of the household. At that time the Chinese still wore pigtails, and the more socially elevated had their feet bound. These physical details may have seemed ordinary enough to a small boy at the time, but when Mervyn came to England it was almost as though the people of his new, unfamiliar surroundings had a limb missing.

From those distant days, in a very distant world, he had begun to write, and to draw, and to be aware that he held within himself the sense of another world, which was not the world about him. His first little book, *The Great White Chief of the Umzimbooboo Kaffirs,* was based on his own childhood experience. His parents were transformed into Dr and Mrs Silver, the surname presumably deriving from Long John Silver in *Treasure Island,* a book he later illustrated, but which he already knew by heart, and perhaps he saw himself as Jim Hawkins. The poems in this volume, and certainly a great deal of the Titus Groan books, also bear traces of those distant scenes, which never left his consciousness even during his long illness.

In early 1937 he rented an ex-barber's shop in Battersea Church Road, which he used as a studio. The house, No. 163, now about to be demolished, is very close to a church which Blake, whom he so admired, frequented. It was at No. 163 Battersea Church Road that he gave me, before we were married, an envelope. Inside, in beautiful longhand, was 'The Dwarf of Battersea', the first poem that he wrote for me. I am still not sure if it is nonsense, but I always felt that he did himself an injustice in his personal references. All the same, I received it with joy, tinged with sadness for the fate of the poor dwarf.

10

In 1939 he was called up, but his years of army life did not put an end to his creative work. He found time to illustrate many books, painted whenever possible, drew, wrote poetry, and completed *Titus Groan*. In that period, too, he wrote much of the material in the present collection.

The short section 'Aunts and Uncles' was written in the late 'forties and sprang to some extent from an evening's conversation with friends, when someone who had just returned from a rather remote country holiday mentioned that he had been staying on a farm where there was a gaggle of geese, and that the owner was hardly discernible from his gaggle. The conversation roved upon propinquity, either between a man and a woman, closely related, long married, or any relationship where each partner takes on some of the other's idiosyncrasies – gestures, habits, ideas – so that it is quite difficult to distinguish one from the other. He wrote the rhymes first, and then added the drawings.

Among his other influences, Lear, Carroll, Belloc, the idealism of Cervantes in *Don Quixote*, the idiosyncrasies of Tristram Shandy, and the world of the wonderfully eccentric English characters portrayed in Dickens were part of his heritage, literary and visual. Mr Pooter in *The Diary of a Nobody* overjoyed his permanent sense of the ridiculous, but he was not immune to the perfections of Jane Austen, the world she presented being equally ridiculous, only more proper. A myriad English poets (Mervyn was no linguist) he could quote at length (and often did), from Shakespeare to Dylan Thomas. I do not think that the writing of nonsense verse or prose was secondary to his other activities, or that they were written as a release from the more arduous task of illustrating. I am sure that they were part of him as a person and as an artist.

'The Adventures of Footfruit', which is the last piece in this book, is also the last he conceived. It was to have been a short book. Its genesis was an article in the *News Chronicle* of 25th September, 1957, headed:

SUB-THINK
SUB-Think
Sub-Think

'They're going to try it on us soon,' the article began, continuing: 'A company was recently formed in the United States with the blatant aim of taking hold of the human mind, without the owner's consent, much less his co-operation. The company is called the Subliminal Projection Corporation.'

The notes which my husband made for 'Footfruit' are included to illustrate an aspect of his working method. In these he hints at his own philosophy, at the seriousness within the absurd, at the dual nature of his vision. In the last written lines, Mervyn Peake seems to be addressing himself directly to the character he created:

> Hang on, Footfruit. This is the real thing. Strap on
> your breast-plate. Flare the proud nostril, blare out
> in your extreme abandon.
> The truth, my friend, and nothing but the truth.

Maeve Gilmore

The Dwarf

of

Battersea

THE DWARF OF BATTERSEA

Ye olde Ballade concerning ye yellow dwarfe of Battersea
being a
true and truftworthy account of hif
death
at ye hand of ye repulfive artift Master Mervyn Peake
when
defending ye moft gloriously beautiful and beguiling
charmer Maeve
in
the year of 'Our Lord 1937.

For ye benefit of prefent-day readers, ye famouse olde Ballade haf been re-spelft according to modern fafsion.

Please turn over

1.

There lived a dwarf in Battersea
(O lend me a tanner!)
There lived a dwarf in Battersea
Whose hands were white with leprosy
(Sing you-O, to me-O,)
And the river runs away.

2

At dead of night he crept to see
(O lend me a tanner!)
At dead of night he crept to see
What he could see at 163!
(Sing you-O to me-O)
And the river rolls away.

3.

And there he saw a maiden fair
(O lend me a tanner!)
And there he saw a maiden fair
With tawny eyes and tawny hair
(Sing you-O, to me-O)
And the river runs away.

4

Then through the letterbox he crept
(O lend me a tanner!)
Then through the litter-box he crept
To where the golden lady slept.
(Sing you-O, for me-O)
And the river rolls away.

5

He gave a most disgusting croak
(O lend me a tanner!)
He gave a most disgusting croak
At which the sleeping one awoke,
(Sing you O, for me-O)
And the river runs away.

1

There lived a dwarf in Battersea
(O lend me a tanner!)
There lived a dwarf in Battersea
Whose hands were white with leprosy
(Sing you O to me O)
And the river runs away.

2

At dead of night he crept to see
(O lend me a tanner!)
At dead of night he crept to see
What he could see at 163!
(Sing you O to me O)
And the river rolls away.

3

And there he saw a maiden fair
(O lend me a tanner!)
And there he saw a maiden fair
With tawny eyes and tawny hair
(Sing you O to me O)
And the river runs away.

4

Then through the letter-box he crept
(O lend me a tanner!)
Then through the letter-box he crept
To where the golden lady slept
(Sing you O for me O)
And the river rolls away.

5

He gave a most disgusting croak
   (O lend me a tanner!)
He gave a most disgusting croak
At which the sleeping one awoke
   (Sing you O for me O)
And the river runs away.

6

The dwarf hissed through his pointed teeth
   (O lend me a tanner!)
The dwarf hissed through his pointed teeth
And drew a skewer from its sheath
   (Sing you O to me O)
And the river rolls away.

7

But look! A creature high above
   (O lend me a tanner!)
But see! A creature high above
Has singed the yellow wall with love!
   (Sing you O to me O)
And the river runs away.

8

And like the story tales of yore
   (O lend me a tanner!)
And like the story tales of yore
This creature leaps upon the floor
   (Sing you O to me O)
And the river rolls away.

O he came sailing through the air
    (O lend me a tanner!)
O he came sailing through the air
For what man dareth he will dare
    (Sing you O to me O)
And the river runs away.

His hair was dark his lips were fat
    (O lend me a tanner!)
His hair was dark his lips were fat
He wore a greeny yellow hat
    (Sing you O to me O)
And the river rolls away.

He thrust a paintbrush through the dwarf
    (O lend me a tanner!)
He thrust a paintbrush through the dwarf
And shouted with a grisly larf . . .
    (Sing you O to me O)
And the river rolls away.

'Get in this tin of linseed oil!'
    (O lend me a tanner!)
'Get in this tin of linseed oil
Before I put it on to boil!'
    (Sing you O to me O)
And the river runs away.

The dwarf turned white but did as bid
   (O lend me a tanner!)
The dwarf turned white but did as bid
And then they fastened down the lid
   (Sing you O to me O)
And the river runs away.

14

They danced a tango up and down
   (O lend me a tanner!)
They danced a tango up and down
Until the yellow dwarf went brown
   (Sing you O to me O)
And the river rolls away.

15

Until the yellow dwarf went black
   (O lend me a tanner!)
Until the yellow dwarf went black
And then they laid him on his back
   (Sing you O to me O)
And the river runs away.

16

Until the yellow dwarf went red
   (O lend me a tanner!)
Until the yellow dwarf went red
And then they stood him on his head!
   (Sing you O to me O)
And the river rolls away.

And sent him down the Thames afloat
   (O lend me a tanner!)
And sent him down the Thames afloat
Within a papier-mâché boat
   (Sing you O to me O)
And the river rolls away.

So one and all beware who wish
   (O lend me a tanner!)
So one and all beware who wish
Within the sacred pool to fish!
   (Sing you O to me O)
And the river runs away.

And all beware who wish to see
   (O lend me a tanner!)
And all beware who hope to see
The golden light of 163
   (Sing you O for me O)
And the river rolls away!

There lived a dwarf in Battersea
   (O lend me a tanner!)
There lived a dwarf in Battersea
But he has now passed over see
And where is he? O don't ask me!
   (Sing you O to me O)
And the river rolls away
     A way
And the river rolls away.

LITTLE SPIDER

Little spider
spiding sadly
in the webly
light of leaves!
Why deride a
spide's mentadly
when its hebly
full of grieves?

Little spider
legged and lonely
in the bony
way of thieves.
Where's the fly-da
on the phonebly?

O LITTLE FLY

O little fly! Delightful fly!
Perch on my wrist again:
Then rub your legs and dry your eye,
And climb my fist again:

For surely here, the atmosphere
Is somehow right and good for you.
I love you most when as your host
I'm in the mood for you.

'It worries me to know,' she cried,
Her voice both sharp and high:
Her dress was yellow as the hide
Of lions in July
'It worries me to know . . .' she cried,
And then she rolled her eyes aside.

Her friend (a dowdy-looking man)
Began to tap his shoe.
His collar was of astrakhan,
His hair and beard were too.
'What IS it worries you to know?'
He said in accents lush and low.

But she had rolled her eyes aside
As though she were not able
To quell an inward rise of tide
And feared to slip her cable –
He turned to where her eyes were bent
Upon a golden ornament.

'Talk not of Fancy, friend, to me,
Though you are old and wise.
My trouble is with what I see,
That's where the mischief lies.
It worries me to know . . .' and then
'It worries me . . .' she said again.

'Perhaps if you could amplify
Your statement, child, I could
Draw from my wealth of wisdom I
Have never understood,
And juggling to and fro with it
Could give some angle that would fit.'

23

'O you are old and full of years!
But haven't got a clue.
What use is solace to the fears
My soul is stumbling through.
Even that ornament of gold
Is quite enough to turn me cold.'

'Your thwarted and convulsive thought
Is mere child's-play to me
These mental wanderings are nought
But biblic fantasy.
You are a whimsy thing and do
Not understand what's good for you.'

'It's you who'll never understand.
You're ancient, cold and blind.'
He heard her turn, then felt a hand
Pluck at his socks behind.
Apparently she's on the floor,
He thought – what next? I'll speak to her.

'Child, child, child, child, child, child,' he said,
'You must not be so prone
To scoff at someone else's head
Because it's not your own.
Your wishful dreams are gaunt and blue –
Your hand has blood upon it too.'

'My hand has blood upon it! O
What grisly work is this!
What do you mean? It's white as snow –
The kind a prince might kiss.'
'A Figure, dear — of Speech,' he said.
It doesn't mean your hands are red.'

'I've always hated them, and now
You've brought them up again!'
'Brought what, my dear, I'll take a vow
I don't know what you mean.'
'Those Figures, sir, of Speech,' she cried,
Her eyes as wild as they were wide.

'I've known them all, and exorcized
As many as I could.
I've had the priest and he advised
I chopped down half the wood –
A lovely wood of oaks it was
Whose branches creaked against my house.

'But it has gone and for a time
The Figures let me be.
Their Speech was all about a crime
I did when I was three.
And now you've let them loose once more.'
She rose and wandered to the door.

'O I must leave you now, and leave
You now for all my days.
Adieu. Adieu. My heart shall grieve
In multitudinous ways.
Though you may have your theories, I
Shall nurse a child named poetry.

'And those dynamic things that lie
Within a carrot's brain –
The passion of the wormwood-fly
That grows against the grain,
If you were such as I you'd sing
The praises of a buzzard's wing.

'I will sway! You are not of
My calibre or clay.
You grope down the provincial groove
And theorize all day.
You're old and clinical and can't
Accept me as a Simple Plant.'

There was no answer, for alas
The wise and cloudy man
Had, like a story come to pass
Directly it began,
And faded gently through the door
And she was left to hold the floor.

She held it bravely, till the pain
Of blisters at her palm
Forced her to leave its oaken grain
And wander to the farm.
The cattle mooed, the byres were clean
But O, what did their psyche mean?

All flowers that die: all hopes that fade:
All birds that cease to cry:
All beds that vanish once they're made
To leave us high and dry –
All these and many more float past
Across the roofs of Gormenghast.

HOW FLY THE BIRDS OF HEAVEN

How fly the birds of heaven save by their wings?
How tread the stags, those huge and hairy things,
Save by their feet? How do the fishes turn
In their wet purlieus, where the mermaids yearn,
Save by their tails? How does the plantain sprout,
Save by that root it cannot do without.
I hope that I have made my meaning clear. . . .

OF PYGMIES, PALMS AND PIRATES

Of pygmies, palms and pirates,
Of islands and lagoons,
Of blood-bespotted frigates,
Of crags and octoroons,
Of whales and broken bottles,
Of quicksands cold and grey,
Of ullages and dottles,
I have no more to say.

Of barley, corn and furrows,
Of farms and turf that heaves
Above such ghostly burrows
As twitch on summer eves
Of fallow-land and pasture,
Of skies both pink and grey,
I made a statement last year
And have no more to say.

AN OLD AND CRUMBLING PARAPET

An old and crumbling parapet
Arose out of the dancing sea –
And on its top there sat a flea
For reasons which I quite forget,
But as the sun descended, and
The moon uprose across the sky,
We were alone, the flea and I,
And so I took it by the hand

And whispered, 'On your parapet
D'you think that there'd be room for me?'
'I cannot say,' replied the flea,
'I'm studying the Alphabet.'

But that was long ago, and saints
Have died since then – and Ogres bled.
And purple tigers flopped down dead
Among the pictures and the paints.

IT IS MOST BEST

It is most best,
Most very best,
To frown upon a welcome guest —
To frown and weep —
O lackaday!
Then to tie him to a hornets' nest
And steal away.

It may be he is nice
And mild
And welcome to a little child :
It well may be O lackaday!
So leave him where
The wasps are wild,
And steal away.

O'ER SEAS THAT HAVE NO BEACHES

O'er seas that have no beaches
To end their waves upon,
I floated with twelve peaches,
A sofa and a swan.

The blunt waves crashed above us
The sharp waves burst around,
There was no one to love us,
No hope of being found –

Where, on the notched horizon
So endlessly a-drip,
I saw all of a sudden
No sign of any ship.

'Come, break the news to me, Sweet Horse,
Do you not think it best?
Or if you'd rather not – of course
We'll let the matter rest.'

The biggest horse that ever wore
His waistcoat inside-out,
Replied: 'As I have sneezed before,
There's not a shade of doubt.'

'I find your answer rare, Sweet Horse,
Though hardly crystal-clear,
But tell me true, what kind of course
Do you propose to steer?'

The biggest horse that ever wore
His waistcoat outside-in,
Rolled over on the parquet floor
And kicked me on the chin.

'O this is lovable,' I cried,
'And rather touching too,
Although I generally prefer
A lick of fish-bone glue.'

The only horse who ever kissed
Me smack athwart the chin
Curled up and died. He will be missed
By all who cherished him.

AN ANGRY CACTUS DOES NO GOOD

An angry cactus does no good
To flowers in a pensive mood.
It riles them something horrible –
O well away, keep well away,
The whole affair's deplorable,
As one might say.

But take the humble spinach-flower
That lifts its whiskers to the shower
As t'were a kind of benison
O weladay, keep well away.
It quotes the work of Tennyson
The livelong day.

I CANNOT GIVE THE REASONS

I cannot give the reasons,
I only sing the tunes:
the sadness of the seasons
the madness of the moons.

I cannot be didactic
or lucid, but I can
be quite obscure and practic-
ally marzipan

In gorgery and gushness
and all that's squishified.
My voice has all the lushness
of what I can't abide

And yet it has a beauty
most proud and terrible
denied to those whose duty
is to be cerebral.

Among the antlered mountains
I make my viscous way
and watch the sepia fountains
throw up their lime-green spray.

THE TROUBLE WITH GERANIUMS

The trouble with geraniums
is that they're much too red!
The trouble with my toast is that
it's far too full of bread.

The trouble with a diamond
is that it's much too bright.
The same applies to fish and stars
and the electric light.

The trouble with the stars I see
lies in the way they fly.
The trouble with myself is all
self-centred in the eye.

The trouble with my looking-glass
is that it shows me, me:
there's trouble in all sorts of things
where it should never be.

CROCODILES

She stared at him as hard as she
Could stare, but not a single blush
Suffused his face like dawn at sea
Or roses in a bush —

For crocodiles are very slow
At taking hints because their hide's
So thick it never feels *de trop*,
And tender like a bride's.

O LOVE! O DEATH! O ECSTASY!

O Love! O Death! O Ecstasy!
O rhubarb burning by the sea!
O day of nought – O night of doubt
Beneath the moon's marmorial snout
Ah pity, pity me!

A voice across the coughing brine
Has sewn your spirit into mine,
O love! it is for me to die
Upon your bosom noisily.

Along the cold, regurting
Shore we passed,
My arm around her irritating
Wasp-like waist
She likes it so.

O HERE IT IS AND THERE IT IS...

Mervyn Peake.

O here it is! and there it is!
And no-one knows whose share it is!
Nor dares to stake a claim –
But we have seen it in the air,
A fairy, like a William pear –
With but itself to blame.

A thug it is! and smug it is;
And like a floating pug it is,
Above the orchard trees.
It has no right – no right at all
To soar above the orchard wall
With chilblains on its knees.

O HERE IT IS! AND THERE IT IS!

O here it is! And there it is!
And no one knows whose share it is
Nor dares to stake a claim –
But we have seen it in the air
A fairy like a William Pear –
With but itself to blame.

A thug it is – and smug it is
And like a floating pug it is
Above the orchard trees
It has no right – no right at all
To soar above the orchard wall
With chilblains on its knees.

I HAVE MY PRICE

I have my price – it's rather high
(about the level of your eye)
but if you're nice to me I'll try
to lower it for you –

To lower it! To lower it!
Upon the kind of rope they knit
from yellow grass in Paraguay
where knitting is taboo.

Some knit them purl, some knit them plain
some knit their brows of pearl in vain.
Some are so plain, they try again
to tease the wool of love!
O felony in Paraguay
there's not a soul in Paraguay
who's worth the dreaming of.
They say,
who's worth the dreaming of.

LEAN SIDEWAYS ON THE WIND

Lean sideways on the wind, and if it bears
Your weight, you are a daughter of the Dawn –
If not, pick up your carcass, dry your tears,
Brush down your dress – for that sweet elfin horn

You thought you heard was from no fairyland –
Rather it flooded through the kitchen floor,
From where your Uncle Eustace and his band
Of flautists turn my cellar, more and more

Into a place of hollow and decay:
That is my theory, darling, anyway.

TINTINNABULUM

There was a man came up to me,
He said, 'I know you well,
Within your face I'm sure I see
The tinkling of a bell.'

I said to him. 'I rather doubt
We've ever met before!
I cannot recollect your snout,
Retire, and say no more.'

But he continued, 'I recall
Our meeting long ago,
Your face amazed me then with all
Its tinkles, don't you know.'

He put his ear within a good
Four inches of the space
On which my features sit and brood
And listened to my face.

'Just so,' he said at last, 'just so.
Sit down, O tinkly one.
Here in the cool our thoughts can flow
To where they first began.'

I said, 'I know you not: nor where
You live: nor who you be
And much resent the way you stare
Exclusively at me.'

'It is the tinkling, sir,' he said,
'Your face is pastoral
Behind its monstrousness are spread
The pastures lush and cool.

'Behind the hot, ridiculous
Red face of you, there ring
The bells of youth, melodious
As sheepfolds in a spring.

'I'm sure I'm not mistaken, sir,
My ears could not forget
With such interior
Melodies, dry or wet.

'I must have met you long ago,
In Maida Vale I think,
When the canal was bright with snow
And black with Indian ink.

'Beneath an archway, on a stair
(The harvest moon was full –
One edge of it was trimmed with hair,
The other edge with wool)

'I saw your shape descend on me –
It all comes gaily back
You stood and tried to bend on me
Your eyes of button-black.

'Away, away, I heard you say
(Just as you have tonight –
Heaven knows I wasn't in your way
Or showing too much light).

'Away! Away! I heard you say
But swiftly I replied
I've every kind of right to stay
The law is on my side.

'No MORAL right, no MORAL right,
You screamed in double prose
You have no case at all tonight
I am the man who knows.

'And then – you TINKLED. T'was that sound
That cantered through my ears
And thence into a vale of sound
Too deep for human tears.'

'No, no, no, no, it is not so!
Your memory's at fault!
How can such recollections grow
On boughs of biblic salt.

'It was not me, for I am not
The tinkling type, I said,
I am a businessman, I've got
A bowler on my head.'

'Mere counterfeit!' the man replied,
'That symbol of the grave
Could never even hope to hide
That YOU are not a slave.

'There is a sparkle in your eye,
A lightness in your tread
And your demeanour crisp and spry
Leaves nothing to be said.

'Give up your soul. Deny your pride,
Confess your guilt, and be
Unutterably on my side
Before we go to tea.

'Though I'm a stranger, can't you feel
Our kinship – otherwise
How could your presence soft as veal
Bring tears into my eyes.

'Turn over a fresh page my friend
And turn it over fast
For no one knows how soon may end
The foolscap of your past.

'Come, let me hold you by the raw
Black elbow of your coat,
Your courage mounts : O leave the shore
While this is yet a boat.

'I am your boat! I am your crew
Your rudder or your mast –
Your friend, I am your limpets too
And your elastoplast.'

How could I fail to be inspired
So hotly said.
I found my inner faith was fired,
The blood rushed to my head.

'O stranger, I will tell you all!
I am the man I was
So nervous of my inner bell
Especially out of doors.

'But I am he : the tinkly one,
What I can do, I will.'
Said he, 'See how the golden sun
Sits on that pea-green hill.

'It is a sign. You have confessed
Your finer self breaks through,
Even the flowers your books have pressed
Are ogling in the dew.

'Sit down, sit down,' he said. I squatted
On the sparkling pasture
The rain came down and filled my spotted
Shirt with pleasant moisture.

A kind of ecstasy descended
With the rain on me
And gradually I unbended
Metaphysically.

Sweet genesis! My tingling thumbs
Describing wide arcs so bright
They might have been those starry crumbs
That thread the arctic night.

And by exorbitant degrees
My body grew involved
Until the problem of my knees
And elbows were resolved

Until my brain grew clearer far
Than it had ever been
That both my ears now kept ajar
Might hear what I had seen.

If it be so, that quite unknown
To friends, I tinkle, stranger
Please tell me, am I quite alone
In this – and is there danger?

He listened once again, his ear
Close to my face, and cried,
'There is no danger – yet I hear
Such silvery sounds inside

'Such sounds as fairies pluck from shrimps
Of starbeams in the dew,
O Lord it is a moving thing
To listen sir to you.'

His ear was very near my face,
I bit it once for fun
He said, 'You ought to know your place
With friendship newly born.'

'I trusted you,' I said, 'to know
The friendly way I meant it.'
'Ah well,' he said, 'I'll get to know
Your ways, and won't resent it.'

He listened once again. I kept
Immobile. An improvement
So great, he said my tinkling leapt
Straight through the second movement

Such dulcet sounds as might inspire
A broker with the thrill
Of consummating his desire
To hug a daffodil.

Again I spoke, 'O tell me, am
I quite alone in this
Weird tintinnabulation, Sam,
Is it indigenous?'

I called him Sam because I felt
Our friendship, strange and quick,
Needed cementing. Would he melt?
And call me Roderick?

He did – there was no doubt a svelte
And psychic power possessed us,
For neither name was one which spelt
The proof of our asbestos.

'Am I alone,' I once again
Reverted to my theme,
'Do other tinklers wake the strain
Of cowbells in the cream?'

'There are three others who have this
Peculiar trait. They are
A grocer bred in Pontefrice
A bison and a tsar.

'You are the fourth and I will prove
Your excellence to all.
Cast off that symbol of the grave
Your bowler and your pall.'

His arguments had been so fair
And what is more I know
That there was really something there
That needed seeing to.

So, standing in the lashing rain
I wrenched my hat away
From my haematic head, in pain,
And then symbolically.

His eyes were on me all the while
I flung the symbol through
The downpour with the kind of smile
That needs attending to.

And I was free! And now my goal
Is on a different plane
And I will never let my soul
Be rude to me again.

THE HIDEOUS ROOT

A plumber appeared by the light of the Moon
And sang like the grinding of brakes
To his wife, who made answer, which, though out of tune
And aesthetically full of mistakes
Was sweet in his ear, for he knew that it meant
She was waiting for him in their wickerwork tent.

The plumber, deploying the light of the Moon
Permitted his body to spring
Like a leaf in the wind, like a heifer in June,
Like a fish, or a ball on a string —
There was joy in his heart, and the prawns in his hair
Felt the wind in their scales as he leapt through the air.

The leap of a plumber in tropical climes
Is a sight calculated to pluck
At the heart-strings of those who, ahead of the times,
Know skill, when they see it, from luck —
O full of abandon and zest in the sight
Of a plumber spread-eagled in amorous flight.

When the plumber had landed, his echoes had died
Through the forest, and he was alone
With his shadow, his passion, his prawns and his pride
And his suitcase from Marylebone.
Above him the trees with their heliotrope fruit
Reflected their sheen on his tropical suit.

His tropical suit, that he made long ago
In his bachelor days, 'neath a tree
With his needle and cotton aglint in the glow
Of a sunset that sat on the sea —
The suit that enriched seven months of his life
In the making thereof for the eye of a wife.

And a wife soon enough had landed on the scene,
She had watched him one evening of thrills,
His suit in the starlight was purple and green
And was garnished with tassels and frills.
On his shimmering sleeves there were crescents and moons
And his chest was embroidered with knives, forks and spoons.

His collar was seaweed dragged out of the sea
All golden and shiny and wet.
His hat was an elephant's ear, that could be
Twisted up like a fresh serviette
That is perched on the table when very clean guests
Are invited to dinner with studs in their vests.

Now that very same evening (the evening she saw
Him appear in his tropical suit)
She had stood silhouetted against the white shore,
In her hand was the Hideous Root –
The Root, but for which he might never have known
Anything could be worse than the face of his OWN.

But O it WAS worse, it was worse than a dream
Of a gargoyle coiled up in a fight
With itself, whom it bites, and decides that each scream
Is not its by some face in the night
Far worse was this Hideous Root, that she carried
At the side of her face, even though she was married

And O, to the plumber, as lovely she is
As a rose on the brow of a fawn.
Or a dewdrop that gurgles in aqueous bliss,
In tremulous light of the dawn.
How gorgeous she was, he remembered that day
On the sands, when he wooed her and took her away.

'But the Root,' he had murmured, 'the Root, my most sweet!
Must it SHARE in our marital life?'
She had smirked like a fairy and wriggled her feet
Then replied, 'You must know that a wife
Has her secrets, my dear, and this Root is my friend –
Be patient with me, though you can't understand.'

The plumber remembered the pride he had known
In taking her into his arms
Though she still held the Root very close to the bone
Which confused the deploy of his charms
But O there was pride in his promise to never
Refer to the Root, though he clutch it forever.

He entered the glade with a bounce of such joy
That the serviette hat on his head
Was blown through the air though he'd fixed it with gloy
To his ears which were lilac and red.
It stuck in a tree and a bird with thick legs
Jumped inside with a bang and laid thirty-three eggs.

When he came to the wickerwork tent he gave cry
As before (like the grinding of brakes)
And peered through the wickerwork door with one eye
To observe the reaction that shakes
The frame of a loving and sensitive spouse
When the cry of a husband vibrates through the house.

But O! the Black Horror! the Sharp Disillusion!
The grim realistical Fact!
She was there, it is true, but was coiled in confusion
And foiled by lack of his tact.
She had not been prepared for his speed, nor before
Had been caught unawares when he peered through the door.

No! Never before since that day of all days
When he watched her against the white shore.
No! Never before, since the fire of his praise
Had scalded her – never before
In his life had he ever had reason to doubt
(O where was the Root she was never without)

That horrible, desperate Ghoul of a Root,
That nightmare of twitches and twists,
That riot of wrinkles from skull-piece to foot
With its surfeit of ankles and fists,
That coiling, incurable, knobbled and scarred
Monstrosity measuring nearly a yard.

As he looked through the wickerwork what should he spy
But his wife in a whirlpool of speed
When she stopped to draw breath he could see with one eye
She was very distracted indeed –
She had lost her Ridiculous Root and he saw
That without it her beauty was never no more

The Root which she held in the grip of her paw
As a foil to her negative charms
The Root that would heave with her every snore
As it lay through the night in her arms
O the qualms that now racked him, the Root being gone
Made hay of his pride in a beauty now flown.

For ah, in her terrible moments of rest
He could see she was frightful indeed
The Terrible Root that had helped to invest
Her face with the bloom of her breed
Was missing! And she, being glad of a mate
Was searching for it at a hideous rate.

The plumber was mortified, hesitant, full
Of deep terror, but suddenly saw
The Root on the grass 'neath the bright tree and all
His confidence flowered once more
He grasped it and cried to his lady within :
'Your Root, my beloved, your Root's in my fire.'

At the sound, like a meteor that streams through a cloud
His mate had burst out of the tent
As a knife runs through butter, she sailed with a loud
And shattering sound as she went
Through the wickerwork wall of their dwelling, to land
By her husband who held the Great Root in his hand.

She snatched at the Hideous Root in a wild
Unladylike manner, and squeezed
The hideous thing in her arms like a child,
Beside her the Root by the rule
Of stark relativity lowered the wood

O'er the eyes of the plumber, and she was once more
An ornament made for his praise
The Root with its mystical powers of yore
Resolved his inelegant ways
And a vision of all that her beauty had been
Returned to enchant the connubial scene.

But now, double padlocked, the jubilant wife
Of the plumber has chained to her side
The Hideous Root which she guards with her life.
For what can more furnish a bride
With tranquillity, faith and a pride in her lot
Than a foil of the kind that the lady has got.

And from then until now the thrice halcyon days
Flow by them, the lady be-charmed
With the Root at her belt while he floods her with praise
In a manner ornate and unharmed
And yet – at the back of his mind sometimes stirs,
A dislike of That Root and that secret of hers.

THE MEN IN BOWLER HATS ARE SWEET

The Men in Bowler Hats are sweet!
And dance through April showers,
So innocent! Oh, it's a treat
To watch their tiny little feet
Leap nimbly through the arduous wheat
Among the lambs and flowers.

Many and many is the time
That I have watched them play,
A broker drenched in glimmering rime,
A banker, innocent of crime,
With lots of bears and bulls, in time
To share the holiday.

The grass is lush – the moss is plush,
The trees are hands at prayer.
The banker and the broker flush
To see a white rose in a bush,
And gasp with joy, and with a blush
They hug each bull and bear.

The Men in Bowler Hats are sweet
Beneath their bowler hats.
It's not their fault if, in the heat
Of their transactions, I repeat
It's not their fault if vampires meet
And gurgle in their spats.

SHRINK, SHRINK

'Shrink! Shrink!' said I
'But why?' she cried
'Do as I bid you'
I replied

And as she once
had promised she
would both obey and honour me

Just me, most just
and holy me
she shrank a bit
for me to see

'More! More!' I said
'That's not enough
I want you wrinkled up
like duff

'For I am tired
of your smooth skin
I want you wrinkled up
like sin'

She then complied
and when I saw
her chin was tapping
on the floor

I said 'Enough!
Now you can go
to your mamma
and tell her so.'

AUNTS AND UNCLES

When Aunty Jane
Became a Crane
She put one leg behind her head;
And even when the clock struck ten
Refused to go to bed.

When Aunty Grace
Became a Plaice
She all but vanished sideways on;
Except her nose
And pointed toes
The rest of her was gone.

When Uncle Wog
Became a Dog
He hid himself for shame;
He sometimes hid his bone as well
And wouldn't hear the front-door bell,
Or answer to his name.

AUNTY FLO

When Aunty Flo
Became a Crow
She had a bed put in a tree;
And there she lay
And read all day
Of ornithology.

When Aunty Vi
Became a Fly
Her favourite nephew
Sought her life;
How could he know
That with each blow
He bruised his Uncle's wife?

When Uncle Sam
Became a Ham
We did not care to carve him up;
He struggled so;
We let him go
And gave him to the pup.

AUNTY VI

AUNTY MIG

When Aunty Nag
Became a Crag
She stared across the dawn,
To where her spouse
Kept open house
With ladies on the lawn.

When Aunty Mig
Became a Pig
She floated on the briny breeze,
With irritation in her heart
And warts upon her knees.

When Aunty Jill
Became a Pill
She stared all day through dark-blue glass;
And always sneered
When men appeared
To ask her how she was.

When Uncle Jake
Became a Snake
He never found it out;
And so as no one mentions it
One sees him still about.

CROWN ME WITH HAIRPINS

Crown me with hairpins intertwined
Into a wreath each hairpin lined
With plush that only spinsters find
At night beneath huge sofas where
The feathers, wool and straw and hair
Bulge through a lining old as time
And secret as a beldam's lair
Of ghostly grime.

Tired aunts who live on sphagnum moss
Are quite the best to ask, because
They are less likely to get cross
Than those less ancient ones who still
Peer coyly from the window-sill,
Until their seventieth year.
Go find an old and *tired* one,
Secure the hairpin; then have done
With your relations, dear.

SQUAT URSULA

Squat Ursula the golden
With such wild beauty blest
That when a man's beholden
Her glory – heel to crest –
He rests – if he's an old'n
It's wise to take a rest.

Squat Ursula the golden
Can tire the young men too,
Because her limbs are moulden
From honey, milk and dew,
And April leaves, and olden
Magic – and Irish stew.

But Ursula has vanished
with some unbridled boy
Along with pictures varnished
With swamps of sepia gloy
Along with bronzes burnished
And all the tripe of Troy.

O Ursula, Squat Ursula,
Wild Ursula, recall
That night I sang a versula
Beneath the midnight wall.
And how you were so terse-ula
And sharp with me, n' all.

But you are gone; your goldness
Your wildness and your squat
Magnetic form; your coldness
That left me piping hot –
And you are gone my olden
Flame whom I never ought!

Along with Saul and Moses
Along with all the lot
Who had fantastic noses
And didn't care a jot –
O Ursula! what roses
I ever plucked or bought

Have been for you, my passion,
My queen of fire and dread;
Divine amalgamation
Of swedes and copper-thread,
Unstitch your irritation
And kiss me when I'm dead.

LEAVE THE STRONGER

Leave the stronger
and the lesser
things to me!
Lest that conger
named Vanessa
who is longer
than a dresser
visits thee.

He is slippery,
he is hardy,
he is hardly ever
tardy,
he can count
from one to three.

Leave the stronger
and the lesser
things to me!
Fish or fowl, it's all the same
to me, all's one and two
and three
for I am now
the sorriest cow
of Capricorn.

My scales are pink
my eyes are black
my feathers flutter
down my back
the firelight fails
to comfort me
All's one . . . all's two
and sometimes three.

THE THREADS REMAIN

The threads remain, and cotton ones
Last longer than a thought
Which takes so long before it's sold
And dies before it's bought.

I must begin to classify
My loves, because of my
Disorganized desire to live
Before it's time to die.

First there's the love I bear my friends
(A poor and sickly thing),
And then my love for all that long
Wild family of string.

Such as the brothers chord and twine,
And Uncle Rope, who's bred
With cotton on the brain, and all
My love is based on thread.

Then there is the love I store
And lavish on myself
A healthy and a freckled beast
(I keep it on a shelf).

So now I know myself and I
Can start my life anew,
Half magical, half tragical
And half an hour, or two.

OVER THE BORDER
or
THE ADVENTURES OF FOOTFRUIT

Footfruit, a healthy, happy man, crosses the border from the wilderness.

He is approached by an official, who seems to have risen out of the dust at his feet.

Far from interrogating Footfruit, the official becomes more and more fascinated by this happy creature and his answers. But he determines all the same to get him into the same mould as everyone else. Because they don't like people being different.

News spreads about him and more officials arrive. They are all agreed that they must do something about him; i.e. he has the wrong things on, and his nose is wrong, yet he was whistling and humming to himself. Only Footfruit's dog is passable. They cannot understand how he can be so ignorant, and yet so happy.

Why did he leave his home, they ask. He had after all enough food, drink and laughter.

'Adventure can be a voice.'
'A Voice?'
'Yes, in the night, my dear friends. I have been advised to leave the border, and stand upon the margin of civilization.'

Not only this, he wishes to prove himself to his tribe when he returns to the wasteland.

Footfruit can see in the darkness what looks like the outpost of a city. He leaps in the air with excitement. Is it not true that he is near to goodness, beauty and love? From now on he must believe all that he reads, sees or hears. He feels that his conversion is at hand. There is no time to waste.

79

Out strides Footfruit towards the distant city, leaving the officials far behind (including the dog).

Advertisements are from now on his Bible, and he will believe without question.

His religion is materialism. The hoardings dominate everything. An avenue of hoardings.

Taste. Food he has been eating is natural, therefore must be bad. Taste-buds are sold in shops so that otherwise tasteless food can take on any flavour required.

Smell. Natural smells are bad. Everything must be disguised. His nose grows big. Everyone stares at it on arrival. Also he has a natural odour which has to be got rid of.

Hearing. Has been brought up to the sound of silence, or the natural ebullience of singing. Finds that music is potted and permanent, and if anyone is tasteless enough to sing on their own out of sheer *joie-de-vivre* they are sent to a reformatory where they are taught not to be anti-social. *As for my hearing, it is marvellously good. No one can spoil my privacy. Not now!*

Touch. Civilized people don't *feel*.

Sight. At first he couldn't see a thing, but later on he felt the Truth arriving, and he forced himself to benefit from all you stand for. It was a beautiful conception, and the dog loved it. As for the hoardings, they convinced me. There have been black moments of course, but what are they compared with this glory? O Science, what a lad you are.

Priests are the salesmen to whom one confesses not owning such and such an article. Absolution is given on the understanding that the penitent will purchase whatever he has confessed to not owning, etc.

80

Footfruit has a very long confession to make. His jaws begin to ache, and his legs grow shorter and shorter with pressure from above. But he knows that there is Truth to be apprehended.

By the time 'civilization' has done its worst with Footfruit he wants to go back to the wilderness. He is to be met by a delegation, and given a hero's welcome.

When they see him, they are shocked at his terrible appearance, but they are told by ambassadors of civilization that he has had a magnificent schooling and they are delighted with all he has done since he left the wilderness.

It takes some time to convince them that what has happened to him is 'good', but high-pressure talk wears them down, and they come to realize that perhaps after all Footfruit is lucky. And they decide that they would like to follow in his footsteps.

THE ADVENTURES OF FOOTFRUIT
or
THE ENTHUSIAST*

Look!

Look!

Here cometh Footfruit, out of the wilderness: a fire in his belly, a purpose in his head; and a nose for the truth.

Exactly.

See how he covers the ground! Hey Footfruit! Footfruit! Where are you off to now? Whizz! Bang! What a lad he is. Can it be that he is making tracks for the border?

Yes, yes, and more than yes. He is heading for the City itself. Ha! ha! ha! Ho! ho! ho! If only he knew.

What?

Oh, never mind.

But tell me, why the agitation, my friend?

That is quite a question.

Let us watch him. All will unfold . . . we hope.

Thank heaven we're in hiding.

Thank heaven indeed.

---

* A short extract of *Footfruit*, reproduced in facsimile, appeared in *New Worlds*, No. 187 (February 1969), edited by Michael Moorcock.

Where is he now?
Yes, yes, yes. Where is he now?

I've spotted him. Aha! He moves like a god.
Which god?
O any good god . . . hallo there, he's disappeared again. Who
would have thought it.
He's half-way to the Border. Was ever man more ardent.
Or with better reason.
Aha. . . .
For he is of the missionary breed.
As for the Border, each footfall brings him closer.
Heigh ho, heigh ho, and the high hills hoary.

Are you listening?
Why, of course.
Very well then.
Yes, yes.

What is it that he carries in his hand – that powerful hand, gnarled by long usage? Can it be a document?

It can.

It is.

Carry it high then, Footfruit, as you stride. It is your passport into paradise.

Are you there?

Yes, indeed.

Some say good old Footfruit, but there are others. For my part I see in him the world's last hope, but what was that?

Only that mangy hound of his. Oh, I could whip him to within an inch of his tail.

And now the rain. Does Footfruit care?

Not a jot.

See how his boots spout water.

See how he laughs. Ha ha!

As though he had no care in all the world. Footfruit the great. Footfruit the glorious.

No doubt of it.

For see, his future spread before him, his past spread out behind him; and in the middle, why there is our friend indeed, with his warrior's head, and his ears like wormcasts.

Sweet Footfruit! There is no question of it, for he's both sweet and great.

Why otherwise should he dream.

Dream?

Yes, dream. Dream of Doing Good. Wherefore his passion to leave the wilderness which was his home?

It is hard to fathom. He does not know himself. All he knows is that shortly after dawn this splendid morning, he heard the call, and he upped and he went.

Confound that dog of his.

He laughs like a drain.

Forget him.

I will try to.

Aha Footfruit. He believes that everyone is there to do him good.

I know.

Just as he is ready to do good to everyone.

He knows very well that the Great City is far away, yet he strides out like a madman.

Or as though he had a tiger on his tail.

Time was when Footfruit spurned the twisting globe. All of it. No quarter asked; none given. As a spurner there were few to touch him. And those who did soon took their feet away.

Do you remember those days?

I do indeed. Why, civilization itself came within the range of his lash.

His gentle lash.

As you say, his gentle lash.

And the cities were like gall-spots on his tongue. But now he knows better. Civilization was all right.

Quite all right.

And the cities were all right.

As you say.

Do you agree?

Yes, yes. But watch that filthy hound. I have him in the corner of my eye. Heigh ho, heigh ho. He had heard stories.

And he had had inklings.

Goat's milk and locusts.

He had put two and two together with outrageous results.

He had been seen, leaning across the dawn, dreaming of the Big City.

He was undoubtedly touched.

No, no.

No? He had an independence of spirit, that is all.

There he goes . . . there's no holding him.

Oh what a glorious, uproarious, bounding beast he is.

Oh what a pride he takes in every stride he makes.

What a splendid picture, Footfruit and his hound, I must admit it. They carve themselves in air.

86

Hang on, Footfruit. This is the real thing. Strap on
your breastplate! Flare the proud nostril, blare out
in your extreme abandon.
The truth, my friend, and nothing but the truth.